Cranes

BY MARV ALINAS

The Child's World

Published by The Child's World®
1980 Lookout Drive • Mankato, MN 56003-1705
800-599-READ • www.childsworld.com

Acknowledgments
The Child's World®: Mary Berendes, Publishing Director
The Design Lab: Design
Jody Jensen Shaffer: Editing
Pamela J. Mitsakos: Photo Research

Photos
Alexandr Shevchenko/Shutterstock.com: 4; esemelwe/
iStock.com: 19; Hellen Sergeyeva/Shutterstock.com:
7; MarkCoffeyPhoto/iStock.com: 8; Narongsak/
Shutterstock: 12; Pamela J. Mitsakos: 11; Phototee/
Shutterstock.com: 15; Potapov Alexander/Shutterstock.
com: cover, 1; rramirez125/iStock.com: 16; somchai
rakin/Shutterstock.com: 20

ISBN 9781623239657
LCCN 2013947251

Printed in the United States of America
Mankato, MN
November, 2013
PA02190

Contents

Cranes can lift
very heavy objects.

What are cranes?

Cranes are machines that lift things. They lift objects up high. They move them from place to place. They are strong enough to lift lots of weight.

What are cranes used for?

Different kinds of cranes are used for different jobs. They lift and move all kinds of things. Some lift supplies for building bridges or buildings. They can lift the supplies to the very top! Others lift heavy loads onto ships, trucks, or trains.

These workers are using a crane to lift objects as they build a tower.

This wrecking ball is being used to knock down an old building.

Sometimes people use cranes to tear down buildings. They hang a heavy **wrecking ball** from the crane. The wrecking ball swings back and forth. It is so heavy, it breaks through the building's walls.

How do cranes lift heavy weights?

Cranes are built for lifting. They have strong cables that can hold heavy loads. The cables run around special wheels, called **pulleys**. Pulleys make lifting easier. Without pulleys, cranes could not lift such heavy loads.

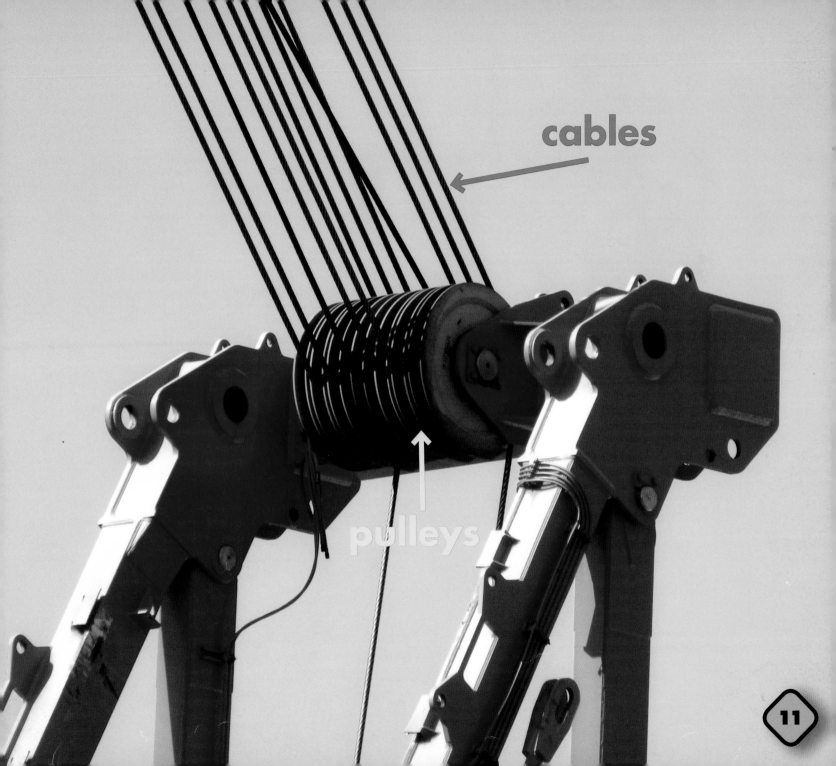

cables

pulleys

11

You can see this crane's huge metal hook.

A crane's cable has a hook or a bucket at one end. Workers can hang something on the hook. Or they can put something in the bucket. The crane winds up the cable to raise the object high.

What are some kinds of cranes?

Mobile cranes can move from place to place. They move on wheels or crawler tracks. They have a long arm called a boom. The boom moves up and down. The crane turns from side to side.

boom

crawler tracks

15

girders

bridge

Bridge cranes let workers move things from one place to another. They have two strong metal bars called **girders**. The girders are high above the ground. The **bridge** is a third girder. It rolls along between the other two. Big bridge cranes can lift very heavy loads!

Tower cranes stand very high. They are used on tall buildings. They have a high metal tower. A long arm sticks out from the tower. The arm is called a **jib**. A **trolley** moves back and forth along the jib. A cable hanging from the trolley carries the load.

trolley

jib

load

19

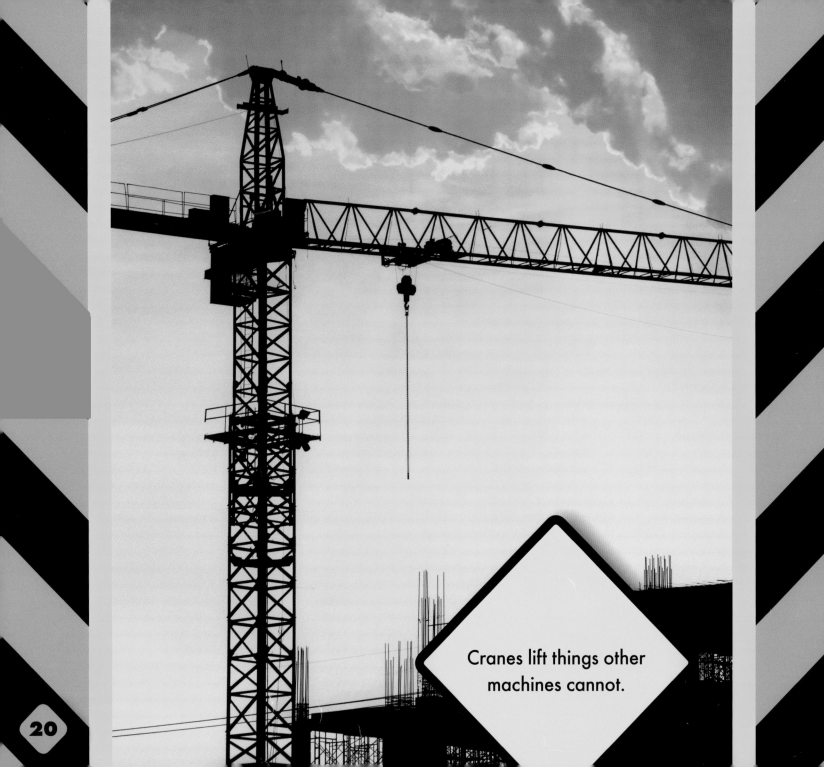

Cranes lift things other machines cannot.

Are cranes important?

Cranes are used all over the world. They help people lift and move very heavy objects. Nothing else does these jobs as well as cranes. Cranes are very important!

GLOSSARY

boom (BOOM) A boom is a long arm that holds something up.

bridge (BRIJ) On a crane, a bridge is a girder that moves.

crawler tracks (KRAW-lur TRAX) Crawler tracks are metal belts that some machines use for moving.

girders (GUR-durz) Girders are heavy bars that hold something up.

jib (JIB) On a crane, a jib is a long arm.

mobile (MOH-bul) Something that is mobile can move from place to place.

pulleys (PUL-leez) Pulleys are wheels with cables running around the outside. Pulleys make lifting easier.

trolley (TROL-lee) A trolley is a wheeled cart that runs on a rail or track.

wrecking ball (REK-ing BALL) A wrecking ball is a heavy metal ball used to knock things down.

BOOKS

Askew, Amanda. *Cranes*. Richmond Hill, ON: Firefly Books, 2010.

Bullard, Lisa. *Cranes*. Minneapolis, MN: Lerner Publications, 2007.

Gifford, Clive. *Diggers and Cranes*. St. Catharines, ON: Crabtree Publishing Company, 2013.

Kawa, Katie. *Cranes*. New York: Gareth Stevens, 2012.

Teitelbaum, Michael. *If I Could Drive a Crane*. New York: Scholastic, 2002.

Young, Caroline. *Diggers and Cranes*. London: Usborne, 2005.

WEB SITES

Visit our Web site for lots of links about cranes:
childsworld.com/links

Note to parents, teachers, and librarians: We routinely check our Web links to make sure they're safe, active sites—so encourage your readers to check them out!

INDEX

ABOUT THE AUTHOR

Marv Alinas has lived in Minnesota for over thirty years. When she's not reading or writing, Marv enjoys spending time with her dog and traveling to small river towns in northeastern Iowa and western Wisconsin.